Original title:
Tropical Blessings

Copyright © 2025 Creative Arts Management OÜ
All rights reserved.

Author: Simon Fairchild
ISBN HARDBACK: 978-1-80581-545-7
ISBN PAPERBACK: 978-1-80581-072-8
ISBN EBOOK: 978-1-80581-545-7

Tropical Serengeti

In a land where the pineapples grow,
Lemonade rivers, a vibrant flow.
Mangoes dance with a twinkling flame,
Banana peels? What a whimsical game.

Lizards sip cocktails under the sky,
Parrots gossip while clouds drift by.
Coconuts laughing, oh what a sight,
Even the palm trees are feeling quite light.

Murmurs of the Wind

The breeze tells jokes, oh so sly,
Teasing the waves that tumble and sigh.
"Catch me if you can," whispers the air,
Plants pirate treasure, with nary a care.

Snakes wear sunglasses, oh what a scene,
As crabs host parties, so wild and keen.
The wind cracks a joke, the trees all shake,
Giggling coconuts, make the earth quakes.

Dance of the Seafoam

The seafoam twirls like a clumsy ballerina,
Tickling toes in a pas de deux, a subpoena.
Starfish giggle as they spin round and round,
While jellyfish strobe lights, pulse from the ground.

Crabs click their claws to the rhythm of tides,
Whales crack jokes, as each wave glides.
Seagulls swoop low, sharpshooters in flight,
Die-hard beachgoers relish the sight.

Swaying to Nature's Rhythm

Giant ferns sway like they're at a ball,
Grasses giggle, ignoring the call.
Fluttering butterflies weather the scene,
It's a raucous affair, if you know what I mean.

Monkeys break dance from tree to tree,
With laughter and whoops, wild and free.
Bees buzz along, keeping time with the beat,
Nature's own concert, whimsical and sweet.

Dance of the Hibiscus

In a garden full of cheer,
Hibiscus twirls without a fear.
She wears a gown that's bright and bold,
Laughs at stories nature told.

Bees come buzzing, thinking they're cool,
But they trip, oh what a fool!
Dancing petals, waving high,
Spin and twirl beneath the sky.

Gentle Rain on Warm Sand

Raindrops tap like little feet,
On warm sand, quite a treat.
They slip and slide, have a blast,
Making puddles, oh so fast!

Buckets come, with toys abound,
Splashing merrily all around.
The sun peeks out, oh what a sight,
As laughter glimmers, pure delight!

Hushed Tides at Dusk

The waves whisper secrets low,
As twilight casts a soft glow.
Seagulls giggle, flying in pairs,
Playing tag without any cares.

Shells gather tales of the day,
While crabs prance in their ballet.
Footprints tell of joy and fun,
As dusk settles, day is done.

Embrace of the Ocean

The ocean reaches out its hand,
Wraps around like a soft band.
Fish in shades of rainbow swim,
Waving fins, they dance and grin.

Mermaids giggle, toss their hair,
While mermen join without a care.
Shimmery tales swirl in delight,
Join the splash in the moonlight!

Caress of Ocean's Murmurs

The waves crash in a laughter spree,
Sand tickles toes, as we sip iced tea.
A crab walks by in a silly dance,
While seagulls squawk like they own the chance.

Sunburns in patterns, oh what a sight,
A raccoon in shades, looking out for a bite.
Flip-flops flapping, chasing a wave,
Mermaids giggle at the antics we brave.

Shades of Paradise Found

In the hammock, I swing with ease,
Bananas laugh, hanging from trees.
A coconut rolls, bumps my head,
The sun said, "Relax!" - I'm here instead.

Mangoes write poems on the nearby floor,
While iguanas plot to steal my straw hat score.
With every splash, the laughter flows,
Even the palm trees join in the shows.

Island Whispers

Whispers of palm leaves tickle my ear,
Coconuts giggling, full of good cheer.
A parrot squawks jokes in bright colored flair,
While fish wear sunglasses, flipping the air.

The sun and the sand have formed a pact,
To keep all the silliness intact.
Tanned toes wiggle in the soft, warm sun,
Jokes float like boats—oh what fun!

Palms in the Breeze

Palms sway and wave as if to say,
Join in the fun, come out and play!
A hermit crab debates if he's too stiff,
While finding a shell that's just a bit ziff.

The breeze joins in with tickles and twists,
Making us laugh with its light-hearted twists.
Jellyfish giggle as they drift on by,
And the sun winks down, saying hi!.

Raindrops on Palm Leaves

When raindrops tap on palms with cheer,
They dance like kids, oh so near.
The coconuts giggle, they know the game,
Feeling quite smug, they act all the same.

The iguanas slip, they're not too sly,
Trying to hide but oh my, oh my!
The parrots squawk, a real fine mess,
In rain-soaked fun, they wear their best dress.

Colors of the Sunset Sky

Sunset paints the sky like a clown,
Pink and orange, upside down.
The seagulls laugh with beaks out wide,
Waving at fishermen, what a ride!

A crab in shades with a tiny hat,
Struts on the beach, how about that?
While surfers chase the waves with glee,
'Next time,' they say, 'we'll surf on tea!'

Beneath the Banyan

Under the banyan, shadows creep,
Monkeys prance, they're losing sleep.
"Who stole my fruit?" one monkey cries,
As the others giggle, oh what a surprise!

A lizard challenges, "let's have a race!"
But nobody moves, there's too much space.
With popcorn clouds, they all just lay,
Dreaming of snacks at the end of the day.

The Dance of Fireflies

Fireflies flicker in a jittery spree,
Doing the cha-cha, as bright as can be.
They twirl and swirl, a shining brigade,
Glow sticks of nature, what a parade!

A beetle joins in, with two left feet,
Spinning around, oh what a feat!
They salsa and shimmer, a quirky delight,
Under the stars, what a dance night!

Waves of Warmth

The sun breaks forth with a cheeky grin,
Sandcastles rise, but they tumble in.
Seagulls giggle, stealing fries,
While sunscreen drips like silly pies.

Children splash with squeals of joy,
Chasing crabs like a little toy.
Flip-flops fly in a sandy dance,
Who knew beach days could be such a chance!

Ice cream melts, oh what a sight,
Sticky fingers by day and night.
The ocean waves, they laugh along,
In this weird world where we all belong.

Once again, the sunset calls,
Fading light as laughter sprawls.
My beach hat's gone, caught in a breeze,
At least I'll remember, "Don't swim with ease!"

Evening Fires and Starry Skies

A campfire crackles, sparks like stars,
Roasting marshmallows from close and far.
S'mores get messy, everyone's laughing,
As the moon jumps in, light's graphing.

Ghost stories told with a dash of fright,
But the punchline's always got us tight.
Chairs collapse toward the flames' embrace,
Who knew bonfires could be such a race?

Crickets chirp with a rhythm all their own,
While friends engage in fun overgrown.
A ukulele strums a shimmery tune,
Dancing shadows seem to swoon.

Underneath the twinkling show,
We find camaraderie in all we know.
With the stars above, we chat till dawn,
And the real comedy is we snore till it's gone.

Vibrant Echoes of Nature

In the jungle, monkeys swing with flair,
Chasing each other without a care.
Parrots squawk like they own the day,
Nature's laughter fills the play.

Colorful blooms dance in the breeze,
Invite all creatures, even the bees.
A toucan struts, proud as can be,
With a beak like that, it's hard to see!

Lizards lounge on sun-warmed rocks,
While frogs boast their own silly tocks.
Nature's rhythm, oh such a vibe,
Every creature joins in this wild tribe.

Yet beware the sneaky vine,
It hugs too tight, it will not be kind.
Nature's punchlines come fast and free,
In this green circus, come laugh with me!

The Calm After the Storm

Raindrops patter like playful beats,
While puddles form, just perfect suites.
Umbrellas flip in a whirling dance,
As laughter bursts from a well-timed chance.

The sun peeks out, a shy little face,
Chasing clouds, leaving a trace.
Wet grass smells fresh, a watery jest,
While kids jump in for a soggy quest.

Splashes fly as the sun comes near,
Each drop glistens with giggles and cheer.
The rainbow arcs above our fun,
Who knew storms bring smiles to run?

So here's to the chaos, the rain, and glee,
In every storm, let laughter be key.
With joyful hearts, we weather the squall,
And find the humor in it all!

Garden of the Gods

In a garden where palm trees sway,
Coconuts fall in a comical way.
Lizards dance, and birds start to jig,
Even the bees think they're quite a big gig.

Grapefruits bounce like rubber balls,
Sunlight giggles as it brightly sprawls.
Grasshoppers wear tiny sunglasses,
Sipping nectar in little glasses.

Limes play hide and seek in the mud,
While mangoes roll like a big, squishy bud.
The cucumbers wear funny frowns,
In this garden of whimsy, no one wears crowns.

But here comes the wind with a blast of surprise,
Blowing hats off and tickling thighs.
In this realm where the laughter flows,
Every plant, it seems, merrily glows.

Fleeting Shadows of Paradise

Underneath a sky so blue,
Monkeys steal snacks, oh what a view!
Their antics are quite a sight to see,
Chasing shadows, climbing up a tree.

Palm fronds whisper in cheeky tones,
While crabs parade on tiny stones.
A hammock swings, there's a friendly fight,
For napping spots in the fading light.

A toucan laughs, with a vibrant beak,
"Quit your giggling, it's time to be chic!"
But all the fish just splash and play,
At sunset's end for the end of the day.

As shadows dance on the sandy shore,
Even the seashells have stories galore.
While laughter lingers in the evening air,
In this land of fun, come join if you dare.

Sirens of the Shoreline

Seagulls call with a raucous cheer,
While the beach ball rolls, no need to fear.
Surfers tumble, it's a splashy scene,
As waves bring laughter, bright and keen.

Crabs in tuxedos, quite a fashion show,
Stealing all snacks as they strut to and fro.
Flip-flops flop with a comical grace,
While sunscreen fights to keep up the pace.

Conch shells giggle in the salty breeze,
Tickling toes with invisible fleas.
The sun slips down, it's a brilliant show,
Even the ocean waves join in the glow.

But when the moon whispers its silver tune,
The sandcastles dance under a sassy moon.
In this realm of mirth so divine,
Every wave and laugh intertwine.

Bright Horizons Ahead

With sun in my hair and dreams in my swim,
I bounce down the road, ready to grin.
A pineapple named Pete sings out on a float,
Telling tales of fun, oh what a quote!

The ice cream truck plays a jaunty song,
While I dip my toes, where I feel I belong.
Bananas in pajamas all wave goodbye,
As I travel the path under a blushing sky.

The squirrels throw parties with nuts on a plate,
Dancing in circles, it's never too late.
We sip coconut drinks with silly straws,
While everyone giggles, breaking all the laws.

As the sun sets low, casting colors bright,
We toast to laughter, under starlight.
In this journey where joy leads the way,
Bright horizons await for another fun day.

Trail of the Sea Turtle

A turtle waddles on the sand,
With flippers flapping, what a stand!
He waves hello and stumbles by,
"Life's a beach!" he seems to cry.

The waves giggle, tickling toes,
As crabs scurry, in funny rows.
The sun looks down with a grin so wide,
While fish dance by in a joyous slide.

Each ripple whispers silly tales,
Of shell-shocked turtles and fishy snails.
They swim and splash, a lively crew,
In a splashy world that's always new.

The beach is a playground, full of cheer,
Where laughter echoes, loud and clear.
With sunburnt noses, all come to play,
And paddle their worries far away.

Resilience of the Rainforest

In the jungle where the monkeys swing,
They throw bananas, just for a fling.
Parrots squawk, spreading the news,
"Watch your head!" as they pick and choose.

The trees wear smiles, with leaves so bright,
Dancing to rhythms in morning light.
Frogs croak tunes in a jazzy beat,
While sloths are hanging, taking a seat.

Each plant glows with its own little jest,
Competing for funniest in the vest.
With bugs that rock and vines that sway,
In this green stand-up, it's laugh-out-loud play!

So let's cheer for a world so bold,
Where critters jest and never grow old.
In nature's circus, come take a peek,
You might need a laugh, just take a seat!

Sunlit Lagoons

In the lagoon where the sunbeams sip,
Frogs wear sunglasses and take a dip.
Each ripple giggles as fish jump high,
While the pelicans laugh with a squawk in the sky.

The crabs wear shells, like funky caps,
Having crab races, with flips and flaps.
Starfish lounge like they own the sand,
While seaweed sways and takes a stand.

The turtles throw a shell-abration,
Inviting all for a grand vacation.
With watermelons floating on their backs,
They toast to fun, with silly snacks!

So come and splash in this joy-filled scene,
Where giggles echo and the water's clean.
Join the party, just swim and sing,
In sunlit lagoons, let the laughter ring!

Nature's Palette on Canvas

In a world where colors dance and swirl,
Nature paints with strokes, giving a twirl.
Each flower giggles in hues so bright,
While bees buzz by, in pure delight.

The trees wear coats in every shade,
Offering shade for fun escapades.
Clouds dress up with puffy flair,
As rainbows stretch with both love and care.

The mountains chuckle as they tower high,
Kicking up dust and touching the sky.
With rivers flowing in a happy stream,
Nature's canvas is a vibrant dream!

So smile at the colors that bloom all around,
Where laughter and joy in sight abound.
In this funny masterpiece, take a glance,
And dance to nature's whimsical dance!

Tidal Melodies

Waves that dance like silly fools,
Crabs play tag by the sandy pools,
Seagulls squawk a motley tune,
As beach balls bounce 'neath the lazy moon.

Pineapple hats on folks so bright,
Sipping drinks with umbrellas in sight,
Laughter bubbles in the salty air,
While sunburns turn skin a bright shade rare.

Flip-flops flapping like clumsy birds,
Jellyfish doing the jelly-nerds,
Turtles chill in their shell-bound chairs,
Hoping no one steals their beachy wares.

In this paradise, fun's never shy,
With waves that giggle and clouds that sigh,
So let's dance 'til the stars all gleam,
In our goofy, sun-kissed daydream.

Spirit of the Wild

Parrots squawk with a cheeky flair,
Swinging monkeys steal snacks, beware!
Lizards strut in tiny crowns,
While frogs leap in polka-dot gowns.

Coconuts roll down the green hills,
Mangoes tempt with their juicy thrills,
A toucan hitches a ride on a breeze,
Making silly faces with perfect ease.

Snakes play hopscotch, oh what a sight,
While owls hoot jokes deep into the night,
Every creature in party mode,
Dancing on the wildest road.

Sunbeams tickle the trees so bright,
Nature's carnival, pure delight,
With giggles woven through the leaves,
Join the magic, just believe!

Blossoms in the Breeze

Flowers giggle in colorful cheer,
With bees buzzing songs we hold dear,
Petals twirl like dancers so free,
In a garden where all want to be.

Butterflies tease with a fluttery race,
While daisies laugh with a sunny face,
A breeze brings whispers of sweet perfume,
As garden critters create quite the room.

Gnomes play chess while hedgehogs snack,
And rabbits hop with an acorn pack,
A parade of fun on flowered lanes,
Cheering each other like nature's refrains.

Though petals fall like charming tears,
They giggle softly, dismissing fears,
For every burst of bloom that fades,
Creates a dance in colorful shades.

Driftwood Whispers

Driftwood lounges along the shore,
Sipping sea tales, wanting more,
Starfish tell stories under the sun,
Of battles fought and lost just for fun.

Shells clink together, a rhythmic beat,
Sea turtles groove with two left feet,
Crabs in sunglasses strut with flair,
While seahorses twirl in salty air.

With each wave, the laughter flows,
Was that a fish wearing clothes?
Octopus artists splash colorful sights,
While dolphins giggle through starry nights.

In this realm where fun is born,
Friends gather round from dusk till dawn,
So join the frolic, dance and play,
On driftwood whispers, come what may!

Life Beneath the Waves

In the ocean where fishes dart,
An octopus plays a ukulele art.
He strums a tune with eight-party flair,
While a crab dances without a care.

A fish in a tux, quite dapper indeed,
Swims past a group of clams that plead.
"Join us for dinner!" they clink and clank,
But he just winks and swims off with a prank.

The seahorse ties his hair in a knot,
Wants to impress the snail, but he's not.
"Just ride on my back! It's a thrilling race!"
She replies, "Only if you keep up the pace!"

A dolphin steals a paintbrush, and oh,
He paints a mural that steals the show.
But when he dives, it washes away,
He shrugs it off, "Another day!"

Illumination at Dusk

As the sun dips low, the crabs come out,
They throw a party that's full of clout.
With disco lights made of glowing shells,
Even the turtles join in the revels.

A parrot squawks a news report,
While a sea turtle brings the snack support.
"Seaweed chips are now the trick,
Crunch and munch, it's a party kick!"

A starfish limboes under the moon,
While jellyfish glow with a quirky tune.
"Who needs a dance floor? Look at me!"
They laugh, floating like waves, wild and free.

As night falls, they twirl and spin,
No one's bothered where to begin.
With laughter echoing through the night,
They find that fun is the grandest delight!

Harvest of the Sea

The fish are jumping, what a sight,
They think they're flying, oh what a flight.
A crab in shorts, he's taking a stroll,
Chasing the waves, that's his goal!

A seagull squawks, looking for snacks,
Diving for fries, he's got no lacks.
The waves chuckle soft, a gentle tease,
As the beach-goers dance, and shimmy with ease.

Sunburnt faces, bright as a cherry,
Sandy flip-flops, oh so merry.
The ocean's laughter, a bubbling tune,
While starfish giggle under the moon.

Seashells gather, a giggling bunch,
Trading tall tales during their lunch.
The tides, they know how to amuse,
In this wacky world, there's no time to snooze!

Aloha in the Air

Hula dancers twirl with glee,
Grass skirts waving like they're free.
A pineapple wig stands on a head,
But mind it doesn't tumble, or it's off to bed!

The breeze brings whispers, coconut smells,
With every laugh, our joy compels.
Surfboards stacked in a wobbly tower,
A balancing act, oh what a power!

A ukulele plays, tunes of delight,
Chasing away all worries in sight.
A lizard joins, taps a beat,
As the sun smiles down on happy feet.

Laughter echoes like waves on gold,
Stories of fortune, adventure bold.
In this land where fun is the plan,
Aloha spreads joy, and that's the fan!

Clouded Horizons

In the sky, a cloud forms a grin,
Looks like it's ready to break into spin.
Raindrops laugh, in a splashy spree,
Wandering birds ask, 'Is it just me?'

Lightning bugs flash, like little stars,
Trying to dance, but they hit the bars.
The sun peeks out, with a cheeky wink,
Clouds start a gossip, what do you think?

Umbrellas twirl, like they're in a jam,
With puddle puddles, they dance like a fam.
Rain boots squished, in a slippery race,
Who knew the clouds would show such grace?

A rainbow forms, a colorful tease,
Sweeping aside worries, bringing us ease.
In playful chaos, life swirls with flair,
Clouded horizons, yet we have care!

Fragrant Flower Serenade

Petals chat softly, whispers in bloom,
Bumblebees buzzing, filling the room.
A lilac sneezes, pollens take flight,
While roses laugh, all through the night.

Sunflowers turn, to greet the sun,
In the garden of laughter, they have their fun.
Daisies giggle, sharing their tales,
Of tall grass giants and whimsical gales.

Butterflies flutter, all dressed in style,
Competing for compliments, they go the extra mile.
The garden knows, it's a wild affair,
With floral antics, floating in air.

A bouquet sings, with vibrant glee,
In this fragrant world, we're wild and free.
Every petal's a joke, every scent a cheer,
In nature's laughter, we hold so dear!

Vibrance in the Garden of Eden

In the garden where the fruits dance,
Laughter sways with every chance.
Bees buzz jokes from flower to flower,
Tickling petals, hour by hour.

A parrot sings a wobbly tune,
As frogs jump like they're on a broom.
Tropical leaves in a playful stir,
Chasing each other, oh what a blur!

The sun wears shades, a cool charade,
As fruits in the trees start their parade.
With giggles in the soft warm breeze,
Even the veggies aim to please.

In this place of vibrant hues,
The laughter's bright like morning dew.
A garden of quirks, a sight so neat,
Where every day's a treat to meet.

Nectar of the Sunflower Skies

Up in the sky where sunbeams play,
Sunflowers giggle, 'Come and stay!'
They sip the nectar with glee and flair,
As bumblebee comedians buzz without care.

The daisies wear hats, all a-swish,
Throwing a party, a daisy dish!
Sipping sunlight from dawn to noon,
While petals do the cha-cha to a silly tune.

In the warm embrace of a golden glow,
Each sunflower boasts, 'I'm the star of the show!'
With sun-kissed petals dancing on air,
And ladybugs laughing without a care.

As the sky dims, they whisper and sigh,
Under a quilt of stars so high.
Their faces turned toward the moon's soft ache,
Even daisies might twirl for the fun to awake.

Beneath the Mango Moon

Under a moon, a mango swirl,
Fruits from the trees dance and twirl.
A monkey in shades throws a party hype,
Swinging to rhythms, oh what a type!

With coconuts bouncing like balls of fun,
All branches shaking, the game's begun.
The mangoes blush as they drop with glee,
Saying, 'Pick me first, oh, come and see!'

A rabbit flips pancakes, just for laughs,
While turtles juggle juicy halves.
In this moonlit grove, giggles ignite,
Each fruit a comedian, pure delight.

As night drifts on, so sweet and slow,
Under the stars, the laughter will flow.
Beneath the glow, the fun will bloom,
Dancing in flavors beneath the moon.

Echoes of the Coral Reef

In the reef where colors clash,
Fish tell jokes in a vibrant splash.
A dolphin flips with a cheeky wink,
As starfish giggle and clink a drink.

The seaweed swings to a jolly beat,
With crabs in tuxedos tapping their feet.
A sea turtle grins with wisdom vast,
'In these waters, fun's unsurpassed!'

An octopus juggles shells so fine,
While clowns of the sea sip on brine.
The bubbles burst with laughter galore,
As sea creatures shout, 'Let's explore!'

Underwater raves are the best of all,
With fins and flippers, we heed the call.
In the echoes of waves, pure joy will seep,
In the garden beneath, laughter runs deep.

Ephemeral Moments

A crab in a hat, what a sight,
He scuttles away, full of delight.
The ocean sings a cheerful tune,
As seagulls dance beneath the moon.

Waves tickle toes, laughter so loud,
We chase the tide, feeling quite proud.
A jellyfish floats, looking so grand,
But watch your step, it's close at hand!

A coconut smiles, wears a straw grin,
We sip and we giggle, let the fun begin.
With sand in our hair, we can't help but play,
Ephemeral moments, let's waste the day.

So here's to the breeze and our sandy tomb,
Where laughter and friendship easily bloom.
In the blissful chaos, we dash and we dive,
Each moment a treasure, we feel so alive.

Catching Sunbeams

With nets made of laughter, we chase the rays,
Jumping like frogs in the sunlight's gaze.
The sunbeams giggle, they play hide and seek,
While we's stumble and trip, oh what a week!

A flip-flop flies, it lands on a fish,
"Dinner's ready!" I jokingly wish.
The shrimp wear sun hats, looking quite bold,
While we're losing track of the time in the gold.

We catch a few sunbeams, toss them with flair,
Dancing like monkeys without a care.
In this circus of light, we let out a cheer,
Catching sunbeams, our fun is sincere!

So let's toast to the rays that light up our days,
With wobbly legs and carefree ways.
We may not catch fish nor win the big prize,
But living in laughter is where the joy lies.

Glistening Sand between Toes

Oh, glistening grains beneath our feet,
Each step feels like a silly repeat.
With sand in our shoes and a wink from the sun,
We skip and we stumble, having such fun!

A sandcastle rises, but then it will fall,
The tide gives a giggle, we laugh at it all.
"Look at my moat!" I proudly proclaim,
But a wave sneaks in, and I'm quite full of shame.

Toe-squishing joy with each little grain,
We dance on the shore, forgetting the pain.
The seagulls cheer on our silly parade,
As we laugh at our mess, our downcast charade!

So here's to the sand, those glistening flakes,
With memories made, much laughter it takes.
Between the toes lies the magic we chose,
In this sandy wonder, each moment just glows.

The Taste of Mango Delight

A mango so bright, it winks with glee,
As I take a bite, it's laughing at me.
Sticky and sweet, it drips down my chin,
With every taste, I'm ready to spin!

Mango madness, a fruit salad fight,
We toss fruity chunks with all of our might.
The juice starts to squirt, we giggle and squeal,
It's a fruity feast, an unreal meal!

Tropical flavors, they tickle my tongue,
Like a comedy show where laughter is flung.
With smiles all around, we savor the fun,
The taste of mango—our day's number one!

So here's to the flavors, both juicy and wild,
Where silliness reigns and joy is compiled.
We laugh as we munch, what a wonderful sight,
With each bite of mango, we're feeling just right!

Laughter Under the Palms

Under the palms, the coconuts sway,
A crab scuttles by, it's having a play.
With laughter like waves, we dance in the sun,
Chasing the shadows, oh what fun!

The parrots chatter, gossiping loud,
While a lazy iguana joins in the crowd.
Cocktails in hand, we toast to the breeze,
And try catching fish that are really just cheese!

The monkeys swing by, stealing our fries,
We laugh as they leap, oh what a surprise!
With sand in our toes, we're making a mess,
Underneath the palm trees, we couldn't care less.

As sunset approaches, the sky turns to gold,
Each story told has been a bit bold.
With giggles and smiles, the night takes its claim,
Under the palms, we'll never be tame!

Echoes of the Tropics

In the warm sun, where the toucans play,
The ukulele strums, chasing clouds away.
With laughter and jokes, we're feeling just right,
Echoes of fun fill the tropical night.

A turtle winks, wearing a tiny hat,
While a parrot critiques our ugly dance spat.
We laughter so loud, we startle a goat,
Who joins the conga, still wearing its coat!

Reggae beats thump, as the palm trees sway,
We dance like no one, come join in the fray.
With piña coladas, they splash all about,
Now, who hit the blender? Oh, that's just a drought!

The stars shine brightly, as we spin in delight,
In echoes of joy, everything feels right.
With friends by our side, and laughter so free,
This fun-loving island is the best place to be!

Serene Retreats

Beside the shore, where the sea kisses sand,
A seagull steals chips with a sly little hand.
We chuckle and cheer as we sip on coconuts,
The sun on our skin, while the sea gently struts.

A hammock swings low, while our friends have a nap,
Then we launch a surprise, it's an inflatable trap!
With laughter erupting, as the air goes *POP!*,
Now we're wide awake, and the fun doesn't stop.

The sunset paints colors, like a grand buffet,
We munch on our snacks, while the crabs steal away.
In this little slice, there's serenity, sure,
With giggles and games, who could ask for more?

So here in this bliss, with waves lapping sweet,
Our hearts grow lighter, with every heartbeat.
In the dance of the dusk, where the moon softly greets,
We'll laugh till we drop, in our serene retreats!

Colors that Sing

The flowers are bright, in a vivid bouquet,
While tossed in the air, a flapping toucan plays.
Colors that sing, in a symphony bold,
While we laugh at the stories that the island has told.

A pineapple hat sits on my friend's head,
With party all around, we'll never feel dread.
The waves have a rhythm, we glide like a breeze,
With colorful moments, we dance with such ease.

The sunset flaunts pink, orange, and teal,
While turtles dance salsa, what a strange deal!
With giggles and cheers, we share a good jest,
In the colors that sing, we feel truly blessed.

At dusk, the stars twinkle, a marvelous sight,
Our laughter and joy set the sky alight.
In this vibrant blend, where the world's ever keen,
We're singing and dancing, living our dream!

Brushstrokes of Sunset Splendor

The sky's a canvas, painted bright,
With purple plums and oranges in sight.
Fish in flip-flops swim with flair,
While flamingos strut without a care.

Coconuts chuckle on the ground,
As crabs hold dance-offs quite profound.
Each wave a giggle, each breeze a tease,
Nature's jesters bring us to our knees.

Laughter bubbles in the breeze,
Bananas throw parties—if you please!
Palm trees sway with conga beats,
Spicy mango salsa, oh what treats!

As night falls down, the stars take flight,
With twinkling giggles, they shine so bright.
Giggling waves, they wink and play,
Chasing our sorrows far away.

Secrets of the Hidden Lagoons

In the lagoon, secrets float on by,
With turtles wearing hats—oh my!
A clam sings ballads, a deep sea croon,
While bubbles dance beneath the moon.

Coconuts gossip from their throne,
About fish who think they're handsome and grown.
Seahorses chuckle in tiny debates,
Discussing the style of their flowery mates.

Sunken treasures with old pirate jokes,
Echo through reeds in silly pokes.
Frogs in bowties, they jump around,
As laughter ripples through the sound.

Night brings fireflies, a glittery show,
Dancing with shadows in a merry flow.
Lagoons are alive with whimsy and cheer,
In this charming spot, nothing's unclear.

Joy in the Fern's Frond

Under the ferns where mischief grows,
Laughter echoes as everyone knows.
The ants throw a fiesta, all in a row,
While cheeky insects put on a show.

Mimicking monkeys swing by with glee,
Plucking ripe guavas, oh what a spree!
Ferns in disco mode—an epic dance,
Even the sloths join in for a chance.

Beetles wear shades, looking so cool,
While crickets chirp, they rule the school.
Nature's comedy, a vibrant scene,
Swaying and playing in lush, vivid green.

With whispers of ferns and magical charms,
Tales of tomfoolery show off their arms.
In the heart of the greens, we all laugh along,
Fern fronds sway to our joyous song.

Moonlight Over the Crystal Waters

Beneath the moon's watchful, twinkling eye,
The ocean sparkles like a pie in the sky.
Fish in tuxedos ride the waves,
While mermaids play truth or dare by graves.

Starfish tell tales of their disco nights,
Caught in a conga with tropical sights.
The seaweed dances, a silly sight,
Waving like a flag—what pure delight!

Jellyfish glimmer, glowing with pride,
Sipping on seawater, they laugh and glide.
Moonlit tides create a cheeky scene,
Where sea critters dream of being so keen.

With the stars in their eyes and wishes so grand,
They prank the night in this magical land.
At dawn's first light, they'll giggle and sigh,
As the sun greets them with a warm, golden hi!

Journey to the Coral Reef

Bubbles rise like laughter's cheer,
Fish in tuxedos, oh so dear.
A crab wears shades, it's quite a sight,
Twirl with twinkling fish tonight.

The sea turtles have a race,
Splashing water in a playful chase.
A starfish poses like a model,
With five arms in a grand throttle.

Jellyfish dance with silly grace,
Their wobbly moves—what a funny space!
Coral castles, painted bright,
Invite all to come and kite.

As we float on gentle waves,
We're mermaids with our jelly braves.
With every splash, a giggle's born,
In this world where fun's our adorn.

Kaleidoscope of Color

Colors splash like paint on sheets,
Monkeys swing to funny beats.
Parrots chat in shades so bold,
Their gossip? Purely gold!

Flowers bloom in vibrant bunch,
While bees jive; they love their lunch.
A panda's trying to climb a tree,
With some grace—well, sort of, see?

Sunsets drip like melted ice,
A smiling sun, oh, how nice!
Dance with hues—red, green, and blue,
In this place where joy shines through.

A rainbow pops like jokes in air,
Tickling hearts everywhere.
Join the chaos, don't think twice,
Life's a carnival, roll the dice!

Fishing for Dreams

With a rod made of candy canes,
We cast our lines in sugar rains.
Catching wishes with every flick,
Reeling in a giant trick!

A fish dressed in a clown's attire,
Jumps up high and lands on fire.
With a belly laugh and a wink,
It tells us tales faster than we think.

Our nets are made of bubble gum,
Each catch a laugh, not just some fun.
They flip and flop, a great ballet,
In our fishing escapade today.

At sunset's glow, we dream anew,
With fish in hats that say "Wahoo!"
In this world, where dreams take flight,
Each catch is pure delight tonight!

Heartbeats of the Jungle

The jungle drums a silly beat,
With creatures dancing on their feet.
A parrot sings in tones quite odd,
Declaring itself the king of the squad!

Monkeys giggle, swing with glee,
While lizards strut, oh can't you see?
A snake does the hula, oh what a sight,
In this woodland party, all feel light.

The leaves chuckle as breezes flow,
Each whisper brings a new fun show.
With frogs in tuxes jumping high,
They're navigating the jungle sky!

From the heartbeats of the trees,
Laughter dances with the breeze.
In this wild and wacky glen,
Joy is found again and again!

Swaying Between the Stars

Leaves jiggle in the moonlight bliss,
Swinging like they're on a dance floor,
Lizards join with a slithery twist,
Shaking limbs that they just can't ignore.

Coconuts giggle when they drop,
They think they're stars with a silly show,
Fragrant breezes make party pop,
As pineapples wear their party glow.

Bamboo sticks sway, getting tuned,
To the laughter of flowers in bloom,
It's a garden crew that's prepped and groomed,
Wiggling under the cream moon's plume.

So let's dance on this leafy stage,
With critters who have no regard,
For the rules of the fancy page,
Nature's folly is never hard.

Reckless Growth in the Sun's Caress

In the shade, a cactus lies flat,
Laughing at sunflowers in line,
Mango trees argue, 'Who's fatter?'
Over ripe fruit, their sweetest twine.

A palm tree bends, it tries to tuck,
Its fronds, tucked in a sunlit bow,
While ferns gossip, 'Oh, what luck!'
To tickle toes where green does grow.

Bananas hang in a yellow spree,
Trying to hide from bees that buzz,
'We're fine,' they squeak, 'just look at me!'
But they're slipping, oh what a fuzz!

Together they shake in sunny cheer,
Rooted in laughter when days are bright,
Their waistlines grow without a fear,
As sunbeams cackle, oh what a sight!

The Color of Lush Desires

Sprouts in emerald get a wild trend,
Top hats made of the finest shade,
While petals strut like they can't pretend,
Waving at bees, their glamorous parade.

Oh, to be bold, is what they sigh,
Even the weeds have poise on fleek,
Feeling like kings, as clouds drift by,
They roar, 'We're fabulous, so unique!'

Berries blush in a rainbow party,
Cherries flirt, 'Pick us, don't be shy!'
In vibrant hues, they get quite hearty,
Sipping dew while the butterflies fly.

So gather 'round for this colorful spree,
Where green dreams and giggles never tire,
In this garden, we're all carefree,
Dancing wildly in lush attire.

Embrace of the Warm Sand

Beach towels toss in a sandy heap,
Dunes beckon, whispering, 'Come play!'
Flip-flops flinging with laughter deep,
As shells giggle at the sunny sway.

Seagulls strut with a cheeky grin,
Stealing snacks that the kids let fall,
Chasing waves as they come rushing in,
Playing tag with the ocean ball.

Kids build castles that reach the skies,
While crabs peek out, taking a chance,
'Is this the best?' their eyes define,
In this sandy realm, we all can dance!

So take a dive in this joyous lake,
Where flip-flops frolic, and spirits soar,
In the embrace of warmth we shake,
A party on the shore, forevermore.

Anchored in Serenity

The sun is on my nose, oh what a pitch,
A crab's my new best friend, oh what a glitch.
My drink has gone rogue, it slipped from my hand,
It seems I'm the anchor that got stuck on land.

Seagulls are laughing, they're quite the jest,
They stole my sandwich, I must confess.
Sand in my shorts, an awkward delight,
I wave at the waves with all of my might.

Flip-flops are flopping, a dance of their own,
A lobster came over, but I felt like frozen stone.
I'll swim with a dolphin or maybe just float,
But first, let me find my lost sunhat boat.

A beach ball escapes, it's flying so high,
I chase it in laughter, oh me, oh my!
The sun sets in splendor, as tides kiss the shore,
Tomorrow, I'll come back, to this circus once more.

The Song of the Sea

The ocean hums tunes, oh what a swell,
With fish that do pirouettes, can't you tell?
A jellyfish waltzes, but oh what a sight,
I laugh as I stumble with salty delight.

A starfish just twirled, it thinks it's a star,
While crabs throw a party, no need for a car.
Seashells are gossiping, sharing their tales,
About turtles who wear fabulous scales.

My beach hat decides to take off in the breeze,
It dances with freedom, with utter unease.
The seagull's a comedian, what a boss,
As it mimics my laugh, that's just too much gloss.

So here I sit, giggling at all of this fuss,
A conch in my hand, it's singing for us.
Life's a little wobbly, there's fun in the mess,
With waves serenading, who needs to impress?

Whispering Palms

The palms are gossiping, swaying in cheer,
They gossip 'bout tourists and last night's beer.
Their leaves softly chuckle, as I trip on the sand,
Wishing I'd taken a surer stand.

Coconuts chuckle, they roll in a spree,
Aligning for laughter, like old friends at tea.
My hat's on a mission, it zooms past my face,
I chase it like it's in an adventurous race.

I build a grand castle, it falls with a plop,
The tide likes to chuckle, it won't let me stop.
My flip-flop's a stand-up, it jokes at my feet,
I dance with the breeze, oh, life is so sweet.

A lizard does yoga, on sun-kissed warm rocks,
While I'm stuck in a pose, sounding like silly mocks.
Nature's a circus, and I'm just a guest,
Laughing at life, oh, isn't it blessed?

A Melody of Ferns

In the lush of the ferns, I nearly got stuck,
A frog croaks a tune, oh, what lovely luck!
It hops like a dancer, it's one to behold,
While my legs feel like jelly, they're growing quite old.

The flowers are giggling, they bloom with a grin,
As bees buzz by, giving me quite the spin.
My hair's a wild garden, full of sweet mess,
As butterflies flutter, I must confess.

A sudden downpour, my plans went awry,
As I dance in puddles, oh my, oh my!
The ferns wave their leaves, they're having a blast,
While I'm just a fool, running in circles fast.

So here's to the laughter, the fun in the rain,
Life's better with giggles, the joy, and the pain.
With nature my partner, I dance like a leaf,
In this melody of ferns, there's nothing but relief.

Symphony of the Tropics

Parrots squawk in vibrant hues,
As drifting coconuts play snooze.
Lizards dance upon the sand,
While piña coladas take their stand.

Palm trees sway with utmost grace,
As tourists try to keep their pace.
Flip-flops clap like distant cheers,
And sunburned noses, oh the fears!

The ocean laughs with every wave,
Tickling toes, a beachy rave.
Sunscreen fights to stay in place,
While sand gets lost in every space.

Under the sun, the fun won't stop,
As crabs join in with tiny hop.
Belly laughs and drinks so sweet,
This is where the world's heartbeat!

Enchanted by the Island Breeze

A breeze come in with a sly intent,
To steal my hat, on a mission bent.
My drink just laughed—a coconut grin,
As I chased it down, let the games begin!

With each gust, the palmettos bend,
While I attempt to jump and blend.
Seashells giggle beneath my feet,
This playful place is hard to beat!

A crab scuttles past like it's late for a race,
While I trip over sand with a clumsy face.
The waves applaud my beachside flares,
With jellyfish waving and casting glares.

But here I am, basking carefree,
Trying to dance with a wobbly knee.
A beach towel whispers, "Come take a seat,"
As laughter echoes—a paradise treat!

Rhythms of the Warmth

The sun blares loud, a blushing flirt,
While I'm in flip-flops, feeling like dirt.
My sunglasses slide down in a heap,
As I dive for a dip that's too shallow to keep!

Bongo drums thump, the vibe is alive,
Coconuts fall, where will they arrive?
The hula dancers twirl with glee,
While I strut by like a wobbly bee!

Sunkissed skin and sand in my hair,
I attempt to rise from the lounge chair.
An ice cream cone drips, oh what a scene,
As seagulls circle like a snack-hungry team.

The laughter blooms like flowers unfold,
As I chase a piña colada, bold!
This rhythm of warmth whispers with cheer,
"Join in the fun, your beach day is here!"

Vibrant Petals in Paradise

Hibiscus blooms in a riotous zest,
Winking at me, "Just take a rest!"
But I can't nap, there's fun in the air,
As beachcombers dance without a care.

The mangoes wink from trees so high,
While I trip on flip-flops, oh me, oh my!
A parrot squawks, "You've lost your cool!"
As I try to dive into the wave pool.

A coconut alas, it's rolling away,
As kids run off in a gleeful spray.
My sunhat's dodging a breeze so sly,
While giggles flicker and seagulls fly.

In this realm where chaos reigns,
And laughter flows like sweet refrains,
I'll join the dance, no need to fuss,
With vibrant petals, oh what a plus!

Emerald Isles Awaken

Emerald isles, sun-kissed and bright,
Where coconuts dance in morning light.
Parrots gossip with gossip they keep,
While islanders nap, counting sheep.

Turtles in tuxedos strut on the sand,
They tip their hats, such a charming band.
With grass skirts swirling, they jive and sway,
Even the breeze joins in on this play.

Boats toss about, like popcorn in air,
Captain forgot where he parked — oh dear!
The fish laugh hard with bubbles and gleams,
In this paradise, everything seems like dreams.

Pineapples giggle, they tickle your tongue,
Mangoes in limbo are all newly sprung.
All in good jest, the day rolls along,
In this sunny realm, life bursts into song.

Reflections in Still Waters

Upon the lake, mirrors of skies,
Frogs in tuxedos, they sing sweet lies.
The catfish swim with stylish gaits,
While turtles timeout at midday rates.

A flamingo fell, lost its balance,
It twirls in fabulous, awkward dance.
The snaggletooth pufferfish wears a crown,
Watch out, dear friend, or you'll drown!

Dragonflies buzz in chaotic white,
Chasing shadows, they dance with delight.
When a heron shows up in its parade,
Everyone blinks, is that a charade?

Still waters giggle, reflecting the fun,
With every ripple, more laughter is spun.
Nature's surprise parties show no restraint,
Where even the statues have something quaint.

Sunlight through the Leaves

Sunlight dapples on leaves of green,
Lizards do yoga, looking serene.
Coconuts chuckle at shadows they cast,
While ants make a line like a lively brass band.

The breeze whispers tales of who's gone before,
As pineapple voices shout, 'Give me more!'
They'll slice up the rum and spread a toast,
Raise your glass to the sunny host!

A squirrel's acrobatics, a comical show,
Stealing some fruit; oh no, where to go?
Bananas roll and giggle in stacks,
While everyone stares at the raccoon's big act.

Sunlight dancing, the world takes a cue,
Nature's stage is vibrant and new.
So grab a hammock, take a deep breath,
In this wild party, life dances with zest.

Emblems of the Tropics

Palm trees wave like they're saying hello,
While the sun joins in with its warm, golden glow.
Chameleons giggle, playing their games,
While clowns of the jungle juggle their claims.

A conch shell trumpets, calls all to cheer,
While iguanas debate, 'Who's the best here?'
With every flip of a seashell or scale,
The laughter echoes, setting the trail.

Crabs in a conga line, side by side,
They've got the moves, with hearts open wide.
Tropical vibes strut their stuff and tease,
Under the shade of the dancing palm trees.

Sunset's curtain draws, but the show's not done,
The stars take the stage, one by one.
In this tapestry, joy weaves its beat,
Where laughter and nature endlessly meet.

Serenity in Sangria Sunsets

The sun dips low, a fruity delight,
Sangria spills, oh what a sight!
Grapes take a swim, they giggle and play,
As laughter echoes, night chases day.

Margarita birds squawk, making a fuss,
Cocktails in hand, who needs a bus?
Umbrellas everywhere, quite a parade,
Under the palm trees, plans are laid.

Coconuts chime in, their husks all a-shine,
Dancing like grass skirts, oh how divine!
Check your tan lines, they said with a wink,
Better than any office, don't you think?

So raise your glass to this silly bliss,
Each sunset a canvas, oh what a kiss!
Laughter and fruit, that's how we roll,
In this vibrant realm, we share a soul.

Harmony Among the Hibiscus

Hibiscus blooms in a jazzy hue,
Swaying to rhythms, just me and you.
They giggle softly, swaying with glee,
Like flowers with secrets, always so free.

The grasshoppers tap dance, quite a delight,
Joining the flowers, their shoes feeling light.
A pineapple joins in, with moves so absurd,
At this flowery party, it's totally heard.

Bees are the DJs, buzzing the beats,
Pollinating laughter, oh what a treat!
They serve up nectar, like liquid gold,
In this floral fiesta, never too old.

So if you're feeling shy, come join our cheer,
The hibiscus are waiting, bring good vibes here!
With petals a'dancing, let's twirl and spin,
In this garden of joy, where laughter begins.

Kissed by the Ocean's Embrace

The ocean waves chuckle, tickling our toes,
As seagulls dive down, striking silly poses.
Shells tell of stories, old pirate dreams,
While laughter erupts, bursting at the seams.

Sandcastles rise, with moats dug so deep,
Guarded by crabs who plot while they sleep.
Their pincers salute, like they own the place,
In this sandy kingdom, we join the race.

Flip-flops are flying, all over the shore,
In this salty playground, who could want more?
A dolphin peeks in, with a wink and a splash,
Join us for fun, it's an oceanic bash!

With surfboards as surf and laughter on cue,
We dance with the tides, just me and you.
So let's ride the waves, and giggle in glee,
In this sea of joy, let your spirit be free.

Lush Life in Emerald Hues

Emerald leaves flutter, chatting around,
They whisper jokes, not making a sound.
Caterpillars clumsily munch in delight,
As they joke with the flowers, what a sight!

Monkeys wear sunglasses, lounging on vines,
Chasing each other, spinning in lines.
With giggles and swings from branch to branch,
In this jungle theater, we take our chance.

Fruit hangs in clusters, ripe and so bold,
Bananas play peek-a-boo, stories unfold.
Ripe mangoes giggle, as tummies do rumble,
Let's feast on this joy, let's laugh and tumble.

So in emerald gardens, let worries take flight,
In this vibrant paradise, everything's right.
With laughter and color, let friendship renew,
In life's lush embrace, it's just me and you.

Secrets of the Mangroves

In shadows deep where crabs conspire,
The mangroves giggle, oh, never tire.
Their roots a maze, the fish take flight,
Whispering secrets, what a sight!

If you find a gator in a hat,
Don't be alarmed, he's just a brat.
The trees wear smiles on every trunk,
While raccoons dance in a playful funk.

So come and join this leafy jest,
Where lizards lounge and seagulls nest.
A world so wild, it's hard to guess,
That every day's a funny mess!

With every twist around the bend,
You'll find new laughs, here, my friend.
So pack your giggles, lace your shoes,
And wade through life with lovely hues.

Paradise Found

In a hammock strung between two trees,
I spotted monkeys stealing cheese.
With laughter echoing all around,
Who knew this joy could be profound?

Coconuts fall like soft-spoken jokes,
While parrots tease the sleepy folks.
A pineapple wears a tiny crown,
Join the parade, do not frown!

The sun dips low, a golden ball,
As crabs perform their evening thrall.
In this land where giggles abound,
I'd shout, "Paradise is truly found!"

So raise a toast with fruity sips,
To silly days and joy-filled trips.
With every twirl and every cheer,
Life's a carnival, all can hear!

Call of the Tropics

The call of the tropics is loud and bright,
The toucans wearing their colors right.
Frogs in tuxedos sing through the night,
While dolphins dance, oh, what a sight!

A pineapple party with hats galore,
Swaying with rhythm, they never bore.
Laughter bubbles, it's hard to stop,
As flamingos play hopscotch on the top!

So if you're lost, just follow the song,
Where the palm trees sway and all belong.
In this silly world, find your groove,
And let the giggles gently move.

At sunset's blush, they all unite,
Making memories till the moon's white light.
Join the fun, don't be shy,
In this jolly place, give it a try!

Nectar of the Sun

Sip the nectar, sweet and fine,
From flowers dancing, it's divine.
Bees buzzing with a silly tune,
A golden feast beneath the moon.

There's mango mischief in the breeze,
With monkeys swinging through the trees.
Chasing each other, watch them go,
In search of laughter, high and low!

The sunset splashes paint on walls,
As crickets join in evening calls.
Together giggles fill the air,
In this wondrous, raucous lair.

So raise your glass to life so bright,
With every giggle, every light.
In every sip we find our fun,
Life's a party 'neath the sun!

Sun-Kissed Shores

On sandy shores where seagulls screech,
A crab stole my snack, what a cheek!
The sun burns bright, my skin's a glow,
But it's the sand that sticks, don't ya know?

A beach ball rolls, away it goes,
Chasing it down, oh how it shows!
With each wave crash, I lose my hat,
Just like the last time, oh what of that?

With coconut drinks in hand we cheer,
A toast to sunburns and sandy beer!
A seagull swoops, my chip's in flight,
This beach life is wild, what a sight!

As sunset paints the skies with glee,
My tan lines rival a map, you see!
But laughter echoes, all day long,
On sun-kissed shores, where we belong!

Lush Canopy Dreams

In jungled hues, our hammock swings,
The monkeys chatter, it's their thing!
With every swing, a daring flight,
A toucan yells, 'You're in my light!'

The jungle whispers with every breeze,
As vines wrap 'round like playful tease.
I tripped on roots, oh what a fool,
The iguana laughs, I'm its duel!

Bananas fall, and so do I,
These slippery peels, I can't deny!
The parrots squawk with wings of flair,
While I just wish I had some hair!

Beneath the leaves, we dance and prance,
Making up our jungle dance!
With laughter ringing through the green,
Lush canopy fun, oh what a scene!

Melody of the Monsoon

Raindrops dance on tin roofs high,
A perfect tune—my socks are dry!
The puddles shimmer with playful glee,
Splashing about is just so free!

Umbrellas twirl, a battle scene,
As lightning flashes, I turn to scream!
But oh, what joy the rain can bring,
A chance for leaps, and happy spring!

The thunder claps, a show of might,
While kids with boats are a real sight!
Our paper ships sail proudly forth,
Monsoon melodies, proving their worth!

So grab your raincoat, don't delay,
Let's dance through puddles, come what may!
In rainy joy, we'll find the tune,
A melody that ends far too soon!

Serenity Beneath the Foliage

In leafy greens, we hide away,
From buzzing bugs that spoil the day.
A nap under leaves, what pure delight,
Till ants declare a picnic fight!

The shadows play games upon our feet,
While squirrels dart by, oh what a treat!
Leafy laughter fills the air,
As piggyback rides show no care!

Butterflies, flaunting their colors bright,
Just dodged a bee, oh what a fright!
In nature's arms, we lose the grind,
Serenity calls, it's one of a kind!

We stow our books, and let time fly,
With foliage hugs, we cannot lie.
Under the canopy, peace we weave,
In this leafy bliss, we truly believe!

Warmth Beneath the Coconut Tree

Under the shade, I rest my head,
The coconuts drop like thoughts unsaid.
I dodge them quick, it's quite the game,
Nature's trick? I should feel no shame.

Sweaty brows and laughter ring,
Sipping juice, the birds start to sing.
With sunburned noses and grins so wide,
Here's to life, let's take a ride!

Flip-flops chatter with every step,
Among the palms, it's joy I've kept.
A crab waves hello, a playful tease,
I chase him down, feeling quite breezy.

So here I sit, in blissful glee,
Life's a hoot under this coconut tree.
With every giggle and every fall,
I'm just a kid, enjoying it all.

Island Wonders in Bloom

Flowers bloom in colors so bright,
Dancing around in sheer delight.
I trip on petals, oh what a sight,
The bees buzz on, but I'm not in flight.

Palm trees sway like they know the beat,
I wiggle my hips—oh, isn't life sweet?
The sun's a DJ, spinning tunes of cheer,
As I boogie with parrots, how silly we appear!

With ocean breeze and sandy toes,
Tails of dolphins peek, as laughter flows.
I drop my ice cream, oh what a mess,
But giggles abound; who can contest?

So here in this garden, joy will bloom,
With nature's humor, there's always room.
For every sneeze and every fall,
I say, "Woohoo!"—I'm having a ball!

Serene Shores of Serenity

Waves crash lightly, soft as can be,
Seagulls dance, stealing chips from me.
With sand everywhere, what a grand mess,
Finding my snacks seems like quite a quest!

Sunbathers snooze like logs on the shore,
While my sandwich flies—oh, there goes more!
Caught by the wind, it took to the skies,
Tickling noses and bringing surprise.

Feet in the water, oh what a tease,
Riding the waves brings me to my knees.
I laugh at the crabs, so quick and spry,
In this sandy playground, I'm free to fly!

So here I sit with a grin so wide,
Living the dream, my joyful ride.
Each splash and giggle, carefree and spry,
Living this bliss as the hours go by.

Laughter of the Rainforest

In a world so green, oh what a scene,
Monkeys throw jokes like they're on a screen.
Bouncing and laughing, they swing so high,
With a splash of mud and a loud, silly cry.

Frogs sing sweet tunes, oh serenade me,
With rhythm that wraps 'round every tree.
But watch your step, the wild is real,
I slipped on a vine—what a comical deal!

Brightly plumaged birds throw a party in air,
With feathers like rainbows, each one a stare.
Their chatter and caws, an odd ballet,
I can't help but chuckle as they dance away.

So let's roam the depths with giggles and glee,
This rainforest life is wild and free.
With each merry echo, nature's great jest,
In this green carnival, I feel so blessed!

Paradise in the Breeze

In a hammock I sway, like a fruit on a vine,\
The wind tells me jokes, oh how they are fine.\
Coconuts chuckle, and pineapples grin,\
Bananas slip into funny spins.\
\
Underneath the sun, I wear shades that are bright,\
Lizards on my toes, they dance with delight.\
Seagulls steal fries from the tourists around,\
While I sip my drink, the best in the town.\
\
The beach ball rolls past, with a mind of its own,\
It bounces off sandcastles, all made of foam.\
Oh, the crabs in the shade play hopscotch with glee,\
I'll join them soon, on the warm sandy sea.\
\
Laughing with waves as they splash and they play,\
Mermaids wink slyly, then swim far away.\
With each silly breeze, joy flows from the trees,\
In my goofy paradise, I'm surely at ease.

Sunlit Canopy Dreams

Up in the trees, I spot a strange sight,\
A toucan wearing shades, oh what a delight!\
He squawks out a tune, quite off-key and loud,\
While monkeys perform, they're the laughter crowd.\
\
Swinging from branches, I spot a fine bloom,\
A flower in a hat, it's making some room.\
Bees buzz around, in a jittery buzz,\
I'd swear they were dancing, or just making fuzz.\
\
Pineapple shirts on my friends, oh the style!\
They strut like peacocks, it goes on for a mile.\
A parrot named Chuck shares his latest news,\
"Life's funnier here when you wear mismatched shoes!"\
\
We gather 'neath leaves, where the sun shines bright,\
With smoothies and giggles, it feels just right.\
The canopy whispers, as we sit in a line,\
This whimsical world makes us laugh 'til we shine!

Whispers of the Ocean Waves

The ocean tells secrets, with each frothy crash,\
A starfish tells jokes, and they all make me dash.\
Shells giggle softly, while crabs scuttle by,\
Waving hello, with their little clawed high.\
\
A dolphin jumps high, with a splash and a twist,\
He winks and he laughs, "Come join in the mist!"\
With seaweed-laden hair that smells like the sea,\
I dance on the shore, feeling wild and free.\
\
Sea turtles slow-motion, in their fashionable way,\
Keep up with the current, but dance, they display.\
Octopuses juggle, what a sight to behold,\
With eight funny arms, they're the jesters of old!\
\
Crab rave at sunset, how the colors ignite,\
They boogie and shimmy, oh, what a wild sight.\
The breeze carries laughter, through the evening tide,\
In this sandy funhouse, I'll forever abide.

Dance of the Palm Shadows

Palm trees sway gently, with shadows that prance,\
They twist and they twirl, like they're in a dance.\
Bamboo sticks are tapping, a rhythm so fine,\
While coconuts play maracas, all out of line.\
\
The sun dips below, painting skies in a grin,\
And I join the pineapples, wearing goofy pins.\
They sway in the breeze, every juicy delight,\
Shouting, "Join our dance, it feels oh-so-right!"\
\
Laughter erupts, as I trip on a shoe,\
It flies through the air, like a projectile too.\
And the laughing palm fronds just giggle away,\
"Don't worry, dear friend, it's just part of the play!"\
\
So we twirl under stars, in the warm evening air,\
Where the whispers of fun are beyond compare.\
In a world full of joy, where the silly takes flight,\
The palm shadows dance, in the soft moonlight.

www.ingramcontent.com/pod-product-compliance
Lightning Source LLC
Chambersburg PA
CBHW072218070526
44585CB00015B/1392